Terminal Boredom

I0487369

Karl Bunker

Produced by:
Brian Wiser & Bill Martens

Apple PugetSound Program Library Exchange

Terminal Boredom

ISBN: 978-1-387-89315-7

ACKNOWLEDGEMENTS

Terminal Boredom was created by Karl Bunker in 1986 is copyright © Karl Bunker, Bunker-Stark Industries. We would like to thank Karl Bunker for his kind permission to reproduce this program and for providing the program itself.

This new manual, produced in coordination with Karl Bunker, is copyright by A.P.P.L.E. as the publisher. No claim to copyright over *Terminal Boredom* is created outside of those portions created by A.P.P.L.E..

No producers were harmed while making this manual, although we did fall asleep a few times... :-)

PRODUCTION

Brian Wiser → Design, Cover, Layout, Editing
Bill Martens → Scanning, Proofreading

DISCLAIMER

About Karl Bunker

Karl Bunker is the founder of Bunker-Stark Industries, a software house known for a number of utility programs for the Apple II computer.

He wrote *Terminal Boredom* as a shareware program that was taking a shot at the computer software industry, at a time when some commercial programs were not worthy of their lofty status and were an affront to the entire software industry.

About the Producers

Bill Martens

Bill Martens is a systems engineer specializing in office infrastructures and has been programming since 1976. The DEC PDP 11/40 with ASR-33 Teletypes and CRT's were his first computing platforms with his first forays in the Apple world coming with the Apple II computer.

Influences in Bill's computing life came from *Byte* magazine, *Creative Computing* magazine, and *Call-A.P.P.L.E.* magazine as well as his mentors Samuel Perkins, Don Williams, Joff Morgan, and Mike Christensen.

Bill is the author of *ApPilot/W1*, *Beyond Quest*, *The Anatomy of an EAMON*, and multiple EAMon adventure games, as well as a co-producer of many books including *What's Where in the Apple: Enhanced Edition*, *The WOZPAK: Special Edition*, *Nibble Viewpoints: Business Insights From The Computing Revolution*, and co-programmer for the iOS version of the retro game *Structris*. He has written many articles which have appeared in user group newsletters and magazines such as Call-A.P.P.L.E..

Bill worked for Apple Pugetsound Program Library Exchange (A.P.P.L.E.) under Val Golding and Dick Hubert as a data manager and programmer in the 1980s, and is the current president of the A.P.P.L.E. user group established in 1978. He reorganized A.P.P.L.E. and restarted *Call-A.P.P.L.E.* magazine in 2002. He is the production editor for the A.P.P.L.E. website CallApple.org, writes science fiction novels in his spare time, and is a retired semi-pro football player.

Brian Wiser

Brian Wiser is a producer of books, films, games, and events, as well as a long-time consultant, enthusiast and historian of Apple, the Apple II and Macintosh. Steve Wozniak and Steve Jobs, as well as *Creative Computing*, *Nibble*, *InCider*, and *A+* magazines were early influences.

Brian designed, edited, and co-produced dozens of books including: *Nibble Viewpoints: Business Insights From The Computing Revolution*, *Cyber Jack: The Adventures of Robert Clardy and Synergistic Software*, *Synergistic Software: The Early Games*, *The Colossal Computer Cartoon Book: Enhanced Edition*, *All About Applesoft: Enhanced Edition*, *Graphically Speaking: Enhanced Edition*, *What's Where in the Apple: Enhanced Edition*, and *The WOZPAK: Special Edition* – an important Apple II historical book with Steve Wozniak's restored original, technical handwritten notes. Brian is also the author of *The Etch-a-Sketch and Other Fun Programs*.

He passionately preserves and archives all facets of Apple's history, and noteworthy companies such as Beagle Bros and Applied Engineering, featured on AppleArchives.com. His writing, interviews and books are featured on the technology news site CallApple.org and in *Call-A.P.P.L.E.* magazine that he co-produces as an A.P.P.L.E. board member. Brian also co-produced the retro iOS game *Structris*.

In 2005, Brian was cast as an extra in Joss Whedon's movie *Serenity*, leading him to being a producer and director for the documentary film *Done The Impossible: The Fans' Tale of Firefly & Serenity*. He brought some of the *Firefly* cast aboard his Browncoat Cruise and recruited several of the *Firefly* cast to appear in a film for charity. Throughout these experiences, he develops close personal relationships with many actors, authors, and computer industry luminaries. Brian speaks about his adventures to large audiences at conventions around the country.

CONTENTS

About *Terminal Boredom*

Terminal Boredom is an illustrated computer game of the "adventure" type. However, rather than the usual slay-the-dragon / destroy-the-giant-robot / find-the-hidden-treasure stuff typically found in such games, the primary object is simply to keep your on-screen alter ego from falling asleep.

In addition to giving it something to occupy its sleepy little mind, you'll have to make sure that your alter ego begins and completes a study of Applesoft BASIC.

Because your character seems to be perpetually on the verge of being bored to unconsciousness, neither of these is too easy. Winning requires planning, careful observation and the experience that comes from losing the game a few (or many) times over. You'll have to find ways to keep your character awake, and you'll have to avoid various sleep-inducing obstacles that are thrown in your path.

This software is Personal Domain (also called "Shareware"; also called "doggone greedy amateur programmers tryin' to bilk a few bucks outa people with their amateur scribblings"). This means that you are invited and encouraged to make and give away as many copies of this software as you want. After all, you purchased this spiffy new manual, right? Thanks!

The *Terminal Boredom* disk image is available from the publisher's site: www.callapple.org.

Starting the Game

```
BUNKER-STARK INDUSTRIES PRESENTS:
   ** THE INCREDIBLY EXCITING **
      TERMINAL BOREDOM MENU(!!)



      <R>UN TERMINAL BOREDOM
      <I>NSTRUCTIONS TO SCREEN
      <P>RINT OUT INSTRUCTIONS

      QUICK!!
```

When you first boot the game, you will be presented with the splash screen and then the following menu. As with almost everything in this game, there is snakiness and an air of being rushed with everything that you do.

From the main menu you can choose to Run the game, Print the instructions to the display screen, or to Print the instructions to the printer.

The Instructions are a form of this manual which although more extensive, still contain the essential information to allow you to be successful playing *Terminal Boredom*.

However, unlike most programs that just take your input and continue on with the particular program unquestioning, *Terminal Boredom* questions everything.

Printing the Instructions

```
BUNKER-STARK INDUSTRIES PRESENTS:
 ** THE INCREDIBLY EXCITING **
   TERMINAL BOREDOM MENU(!!)



     <R>UN TERMINAL BOREDOM
     <I>NSTRUCTIONS TO SCREEN
     <P>RINT OUT INSTRUCTIONS

     <█> PRESS <RETURN>, UNLESS
         YOU'VE GOOFED, AND THIS
         AIN'T WHAT YOU WANT.
```

When you choose to print the instructions, you have the choice of
either printing them to the Display or to the Printer. But really, why
would you want to print the instructions when they are contained in
this very "beautiful" manual you are holding? Don't you know that
multiple someones spent a lot of time just for you? That's okay, we
like nostalgia too.

If you choose to print them to the display, they will be printed using a
screen control feature that allows you to display a portion, read it and
continue to the next page.

The controller software has three commands that allow reading and re-
reading of the manual included on the disk:

RETURN	Continue to the next Page
SPACE	Go Back to the Previous Page
ESC	Return to the Main Menu

```
WELCOME TO TERMINAL BOREDOM!

This disk is Personal Domain (also
called "Shareware"; also called
"doggone greedy amateur programmers
tryin' to bilk a few bucks outa people
with their amateur scribblings"). This
means that you are invited and
encouraged to make and give away as
many copies of this disk as you want.
<RETURN> FOR NEXT PAGE; <SPACE> FOR
PREVIOUS PAGE; <ESC> TO RETURN TO MENU
```

If you choose to print the instructions to the Printer, you will be
presented with a completely different screen asking for the slot of your
printer.

Ordinarily, this will be Slot 1 on most Apple II computers, unless you
have specifically put it in a different slot. If you want to just print it to
the Display in 80 column mode, choosing Slot 3 will do just that.

```
PRINTOUT SINGLE OR DOUBLE SPACED? S/D




GET YOUR PRINTER READY (PRINTER HEAD
SHOULD BE ABOUT 1/2 INCH BELOW TOP OF
PAPER), AND PRESS <RETURN>, PLEASE.※
```

Once you Choose the slot and continue, you will then be asked whether you want Single or Double spaced printouts. If you are printing to Paper and want to conserve paper, choose Single space. The entire document is only 3 pages long on the disk.

The program is set up for a Single Sheet Feed Printer as shown in the following Screen.

You can still use a regular Dot Matrix Printer by pressing RETURN at each prompt.

When your printout has completed, the program will return you to the main menu of the program.

```
WHEN YOUR PRINTER STOPS, FEED IN THE
NEXT SHEET OF PAPER AND PRESS <RETURN>,
PLEASE.
```

Playing the Game

When you choose Run the program, the computer will give you the main *Terminal Boredom* splash screen and await your pressing the RETURN key.

Next the computer will lay out the story with the main adventure introduction screen.

While playing *Terminal Boredom*, you'll find a list of the options that are currently open to you listed on the right-hand side of the text screen.

To play the game, you simply type in one of these options and watch how the game responds. "GO TO _ _ " is almost always listed, and indicates that you have the option of going to various places or objects.

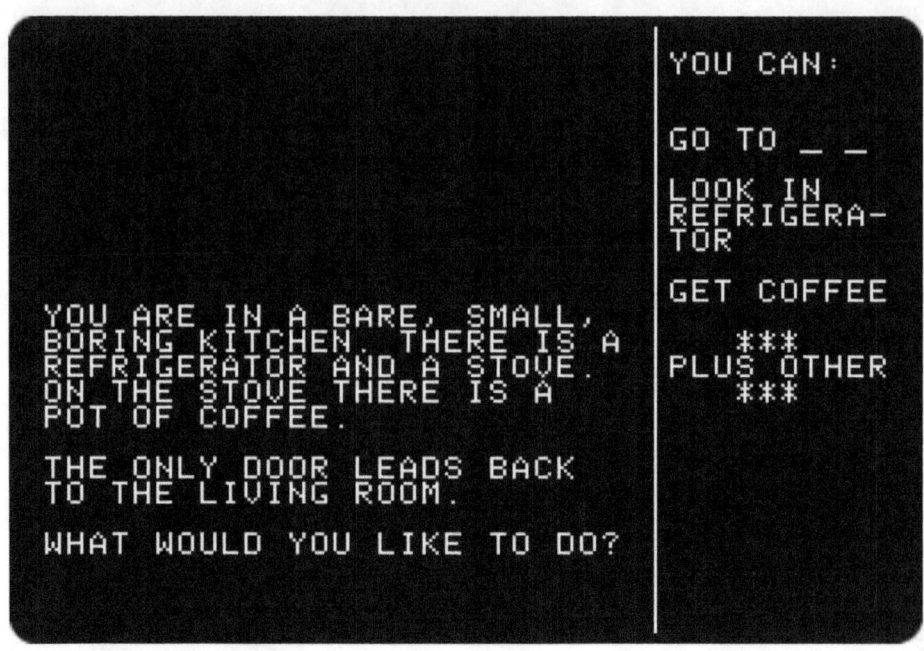

```
                                         YOU CAN:

                                         GO TO _ _

                                         LOOK IN
                                         REFRIGERA-
                                         TOR

                                         GET COFFEE
  YOU ARE IN A BARE, SMALL,
  BORING KITCHEN. THERE IS A                ***
  REFRIGERATOR AND A STOVE.             PLUS OTHER
  ON THE STOVE THERE IS A                   ***
  POT OF COFFEE.

  THE ONLY DOOR LEADS BACK
  TO THE LIVING ROOM.

  WHAT WOULD YOU LIKE TO DO?
```

The game opens with your character at his computer, which is in the living room. If you leave the computer (to "GO TO WINDOW", for example), you can get back by entering either "GO TO COMPUTER" or "GO TO DESK".

If you leave the living room, you can return with "GO TO LIVING ROOM", "GO TO COMPUTER" or "GO TO DESK". All other things/places that you can GO TO from your current position are named when you enter "LOOK AROUND".

Sometimes you will see "PLUS OTHER" listed as an option. This indicates that certain "hidden" options are open. Usually you can find out what they are by "LOOKing AROUND". Because the action (this is "action" ??) in *Terminal Boredom* is confined to three rooms, you shouldn't need a map to keep track of where you are. You might find it helpful, however, to take notes on the sequence of things you do each time you play.

When the game responds with the "Sorry, I can't decipher your input…" message, it means one of the following:

(1) You may have tried to do something that isn't allowed at your present position in the game. For example, you can't "GET" something that's in the bedroom if you're in the living room. You may have tried to do something that you're in the living room.

(2) You may have tried to do something that isn't allowed in the game at all. (You can't catch a plane to Bermuda, for example.) Or you may simply have made a typing mistake. *Terminal Boredom* is a pretty quick little game as computer adventure games go. Unless you're a very slow typist, playing the game through to a "lose" situation will take minutes, rather than hours, or days, weeks, months . . .

As for how long it will take to find your way through to a "win" . . . well, that all depends. There's more than one way to win at *Terminal Boredom* – there's a bunch of ways to lose. If you decide you've had enough and want end it all, just type in something ending with "SLEEP".

A "female protagonist" version of *Terminal Boredom* may be available by the time you read this.

Really Boring Technical Stuff

Terminal Boredom will run on Apple II family computers. Because it uses a "moved" DOS (loaded into the top 16K RAM or Language Card), it requires at least 64K, and Applesoft in ROM.

If you should find a bug on this disk and can describe it, and it's one that I haven't already fixed, or if you give me a suggestion for improving *Terminal Boredom* that I decide to use, I'll reward you with some praise and gratitude.

On the other hand, if your copy of this disk crashes or is otherwise seriously screwed up, it's probably because someone has tinkered with it in some way. (It worked okay when it left my hands, honest!)

To prevent any casual cheating, *Terminal Boredom* is (slightly) protected against LISTing. If you're going to cheat, you'll have to put some forethought into it.

This disk contains a high-speed operating system called *Diversi-DOS*(tm), which is licensed for use with this program only.

And of course, *Terminal Boredom* is copyrighted, 1986; Karl Bunker, Bunker-Stark Industries. No warranties, express or implied, blah, blah, blah, etc., etc.

Tally ho; happy boredom!

YOU ARE IN A BARE, SMALL, BORING
KITCHEN. THERE IS A REFRIGERATOR AND A
STOVE. ON THE STOVE THERE IS A POT OF
COFFEE.

Source Code

HELLO.BAS

```
5  IF  PEEK (55) < 191 GOTO 25
10  PRINT : PRINT  CHR$ (4)"BLOAD PK,A25000": PRINT
CHR$ (4)"BLOAD BSI"
15  CALL 25000: POKE 49234,0: POKE 49239,0: POKE
49232,0: POKE 40286,102: POKE 40287,213: POKE 103,1:
POKE 104,96: POKE 24576,0
20  FOR I = 1 TO 4000: NEXT : PRINT  CHR$ (4)"RUN
MENU.DOCS"
25  HOME : VTAB 5: PRINT  CHR$ (7); CHR$ (7)"THIS DISK
USES A 'MOVED' DOS AND RE-   QUIRES 64K WITH A 16K RAM
CARD IN SLOT 0AND APPLESOFT ROM ON THE MOTHERBOARD.
30  PRINT : PRINT "ACCORDING TO A 'PEEK' THIS PROGRAM
JUST DID, THE DOS HASN'T BEEN SUCCESSFULLY   'MOVED'."
35  PRINT : PRINT "IF YOUR MACHINE IS A II+ WITH THE
CONFIGURATION DESCRIBED ABOVE, OR IS A  IIE, IIC, OR
IIGS (LUCKY YOU), AND YOU  ARE READING THIS MESSAGE, ";
40  PRINT "THEN SOME BOZOMUST HAVE CHANGED THE DOS ON
THIS DISK. 'TERMINAL BOREDOM' WON'T WORK WITHOUT    THE
MOVED DOS.
45  PRINT : PRINT "PRESS <RETURN> AND SELECT <I> FROM
THE  MENU TO FIND OUT ABOUT GETTING A WORKINGCOPY OF
THIS DISK."
50  PRINT : PRINT "(<ESC> REBOOTS)"
55  GET G$: IF  ASC (G$) = 13 THEN  PRINT : PRINT  CHR$
(4)"RUN MENU.DOCS"
60  IF  ASC (G$) = 27 THEN  CALL  - 1370
65  IF  ASC (G$) = 2 THEN  END
70  GOTO 55
```

MENU.DOCS.BAS

```
5   DIM A$(198):N = 198
10  TEXT : HOME :D$ =  CHR$ (4)
15  INVERSE : HTAB 2: VTAB 2: PRINT  SPC( 38)
20  FOR I = 1 TO 7: HTAB 2: PRINT " ";: HTAB 39: PRINT "
": NEXT
25  HTAB 2: PRINT  SPC( 38): NORMAL
30  HTAB 4: VTAB 4: PRINT "BUNKER-STARK INDUSTRIES
PRESENTS:"
35  HTAB 6: VTAB 6: PRINT "** THE INCREDIBLY EXCITING
**"
40  HTAB 8: VTAB 8: PRINT "TERMINAL BOREDOM MENU(!!)"
45  HTAB 9: VTAB 14: PRINT "<R>UN TERMINAL BOREDOM":
PRINT
50  HTAB 9: PRINT "<I>NSTRUCTIONS TO SCREEN": PRINT
55  HTAB 9: PRINT "<P>RINT OUT INSTRUCTIONS": PRINT
60  B$(0) = "CHOOSE!":B$(1) = "QUICK!!":B$(2) = "HURRY!!"
65  Q$(1) = "?":Q$(0) =  CHR$ (127): IF  PEEK (64435) <
> 6 THEN Q$(0) = " "
70  POKE 49168,0
75  HTAB 9: VTAB 21: CALL  - 868: PRINT B$(C)
80  FOR I = 1 TO 10:K =  PEEK (49152): IF K > 128 GOTO
115
85  NEXT
90  HTAB 9: VTAB 21: CALL  - 868: HTAB 17: PRINT "<"Q$
(Q)">"
95  FOR I = 1 TO 10:K =  PEEK (49152): IF K > 128 GOTO
115
100  NEXT
105 Q = (Q = 0) * 1:C = C + 1: IF C = 3 THEN C = 0
110  GOTO 75
115 K = K - 128: IF K > 90 THEN K = K - 32
120  IF K < > 82 AND K < > 73 AND K < > 80 GOTO 70
125  HTAB 9: VTAB 21: PRINT "<";: INVERSE : PRINT  CHR$
(K);: NORMAL : PRINT ">";
130  PRINT " PRESS <RETURN>, UNLESS": HTAB 13: PRINT
"YOU'VE GOOFED, AND THIS"
135  HTAB 13: VTAB 23: PRINT "AIN'T WHAT YOU WANT.";
140  POKE 49168,0: GET G$: IF  ASC (G$) = 13 GOTO 150
145  HTAB 9: VTAB 21: CALL  - 958: GOTO 70
```

```
150   IF K = 82 THEN   POKE 103,1: POKE 104,96: POKE
24576,0: PRINT : PRINT D$"RUN TERMINAL.BOREDOM"
155   IF K = 80 GOTO 250
160   REM
SCREEN DOC.S

165   IF  PEEK (64435) <  > 6 THEN CN$ =
"001600001661121771112011271760082010971440040412231451 1
12002082392281122080052301120760040031981120 96": FOR I =
1 TO 33: POKE 767 + I, VAL ( MID$ (CN$,I * 3,3)):
NEXT :UC = 1
170 I = 0: HOME : IF  NOT FL THEN FL = 1: GOSUB 420:
HOME
175   VTAB 23: HTAB 2: INVERSE : PRINT " <RETURN> FOR
NEXT PAGE; <SPACE> FOR   ": HTAB 2: PRINT "PREVIOUS PAGE;
<ESC> TO RETURN TO MENU";
180   POKE 35,22: NORMAL :K = 141: GOTO 190
185 K =  PEEK (49152): IF K < 128 GOTO 185
190   POKE 49168,0:K = K - 128
195   IF K = 32 AND I > 10 THEN I = I - L - 1:L = 9
200   IF K = 13 AND I = N THEN K = 27
205   IF K = 13 AND I < N THEN I = I + 10:L = 9
210   IF K = 13 AND I > N THEN L = 10 - (I - N + 1):I = N
215   IF K = 27 GOTO 10
220   HOME :VT = 3: IF UC THEN   GOSUB 235: GOTO 185
225   FOR J = I - L TO I: VTAB VT: PRINT A$(J):VT = VT +
2: NEXT
230   GOTO 185
235   REM
UPPER CASE SCREENER
240 F1 =  PEEK (111):F2 =  PEEK (112):JU = 0: FOR J = I
- L TO I:JU = JU + 1:UC$(JU) = A$(J) + "": NEXT : CALL
768: POKE 111,F1: POKE 112,F2
245   FOR J = 1 TO JU: VTAB VT: PRINT UC$(J):VT = VT + 2:
NEXT : RETURN
250   REM
PRINT DOC.S

255   HOME : IF  NOT FL THEN   GOSUB 420
260 FL = 0:PS = 1: IF  PEEK (64435) = 6 AND   PEEK
(64448) = 0 GOTO 275
265   HOME : VTAB 10: INPUT "PLEASE ENTER YOUR PRINTER
SLOT NUMBER ";P$
```

17

```
270 PS =  VAL (P$): IF PS < 1 OR PS > 7 GOTO 265
275   HOME : VTAB 8: PRINT " PRINTOUT SINGLE OR DOUBLE
SPACED? S/D ";: GET SP$: PRINT
280 SP$ =  CHR$ ( ASC (SP$) - 32 * ( ASC (SP$) > 96)):
IF SP$ <  > "S" AND SP$ <  > "D" GOTO 275
285   VTAB 15: INPUT " GET YOUR PRINTER READY (PRINTER
HEAD
 SHOULD BE ABOUT 1/2 INCH BELOW TOP OF
 PAPER), AND PRESS <RETURN>, PLEASE.";R$
290 I = 1:P = 1:LN = 0:LI$ = ""
295   REM
START PAGE
300   HOME : VTAB 10: FLASH : PRINT "- PRINTER NOT
CONNECTED -": NORMAL
305   PRINT D$"PR#"PS: PRINT : PRINT D$"PR#0": HOME
310   VTAB 10: PRINT "PRINTING PAGE "P
315   POKE 32,0: POKE 33,1: POKE 34,23: POKE 35,24: PRINT
D$"PR#"PS
320   PRINT  SPC( 36)"Page "P: PRINT : PRINT : PRINT
325   REM
ASSEMBLE LINE
330   IF I = N + 1 AND  LEN (LI$) < 70 THEN PR$ = LI$:LI$
= "": GOSUB 400: GOTO 370
335   IF  RIGHT$ (A$(I),2) = "  " THEN PR$ = LI$: GOSUB
400:LI$ = "": IF I <  = N THEN PR$ = A$(I):I = I + 1:
GOSUB 400: GOTO 370
340   IF  RIGHT$ (A$(I),1) <  > "-" THEN A$(I) = A$(I) +
" "
345   IF  RIGHT$ (A$(I),2) = " -" THEN A$(I) = A$(I) + "
"
350 LI$ = LI$ + A$(I):I = I + 1: IF  LEN (LI$) < 70 GOTO
325
355   REM
70 COLUMN WORD-WRAP
360   FOR CH = 70 TO 5 STEP  - 1: IF  MID$ (LI$,CH,1) <
> " " AND  MID$ (LI$,CH - 1,1) <  > "-" THEN  NEXT
365 PR$ =  LEFT$ (LI$,CH - 1):LI$ =  MID$ (LI$,CH + 1 *
( MID$ (LI$,CH,1) = " ")): GOSUB 400
370   REM
PAGE FILLED OR DOC. COMPLETED?
375   IF I = N + 1 AND LI$ = "" THEN  PRINT D$"PR#0":
GOTO 10
380   IF LN < 53 GOTO 325
```

```
385  PRINT D$"PR#0": TEXT : HOME : VTAB 10: POKE 49168,0
390  INPUT " WHEN YOUR PRINTER STOPS, FEED IN THE
 NEXT SHEET OF PAPER AND PRESS <RETURN>,
 PLEASE.";R$
395 LN = 0:P = P + 1: GOTO 295
400  REM
PRINT LINE
405  IF PR$ = "" THEN  RETURN
410  HTAB 9: PRINT PR$: IF SP$ = "D" THEN  PRINT :LN =
LN + 1
415 LN = LN + 1: RETURN
420  REM
STRINGS

425  VTAB 10: PRINT " JUST A SECOND . . ."
500 A$(1) = "WELCOME TO TERMINAL BOREDOM!":A$(2) = "   "
501 A$(3) = "This disk is Personal Domain (also":A$(4) =
"called " +  CHR$ (34) + "Shareware" +  CHR$ (34) + ";
also called"
502 A$(5) = "" +  CHR$ (34) + "doggone greedy amateur
programmers":A$(6) = "tryin' to bilk a few bucks outa
people"
503 A$(7) = "with their amateur scribblings" +  CHR$
(34) + "). This":A$(8) = "means that you are invited
and"
504 A$(9) = "encouraged to make and give away as":A$(10)
= "many copies of this disk as you want."
505 A$(11) = "However, if you like the thing and":A$(12)
= "intend to keep a copy of it, you are"
506 A$(13) = "cordially asked to send the
miniscule":A$(14) = "sum of $5.00 to the address below.
When"
507 A$(15) = "you do so, mention the disk title
and":A$(16) = "the version number that's shown above"
508 A$(17) = "the address. If a more recent
version":A$(18) = "of Terminal Boredom is available when
I"
509 A$(19) = "get your five bucks, I'll send you
a":A$(20) = "copy of it, no additional charge."
510 A$(21) = "   ":A$(22) = "TERMINAL BOREDOM  version
2.3  "
511 A$(23) = "Karl Bunker  ":A$(24) = "321 S. Huntington
Ave.  "
```

```
512 A$(25) = "Boston, MA 02130  ":A$(26) = "    "
513 A$(27) = "ABOUT TERMINAL BOREDOM:  ":A$(28) =
"Terminal Boredom is an illustrated"
514 A$(29) = "computer game of the " +  CHR$ (34) +
"adventure" +  CHR$ (34) + " type.":A$(30) = "However,
rather than the usual slay-"
515 A$(31) = "the-dragon/destroy-the-giant-":A$(32) =
"robot/find-the-hidden-treasure stuff"
516 A$(33) = "typically found in such games, the":A$(34)
= "primary object of Terminal Boredom is"
517 A$(35) = "simply to keep your on-screen alter
ego":A$(36) = "from falling asleep. In addition, to"
518 A$(37) = "give him something to occupy his
sleepy":A$(38) = "little mind, you'll have to see to it"
519 A$(39) = "that he begins and completes a study
of":A$(40) = "Applesoft(tm) BASIC. Because he seems"
520 A$(41) = "to be perpetually on the verge of
being":A$(42) = "bored to unconsciousness, neither of"
521 A$(43) = "these is too easy. To win requires":A$(44)
= "planning, careful observation and the"
522 A$(45) = "experience that comes from losing
the":A$(46) = "game a few (or many) times over. You'll"
523 A$(47) = "have to find ways to keep your":A$(48) =
"character awake, and you'll have to"
524 A$(49) = "avoid various sleep-inducing obstacles":A$
(50) = "that are thrown in his path. "
525 A$(51) = "  ":A$(52) = "While playing Terminal
Boredom, you'll"
526 A$(53) = "find a list of the options that
are":A$(54) = "currently open to you listed on the"
527 A$(55) = "right-hand side of the text screen. To":A$
(56) = "play, you simply type in one of these"
528 A$(57) = "options and watch how the game":A$(58) =
"responds. " +  CHR$ (34) + "GO TO _ _ " +  CHR$ (34) +
" is almost always"
529 A$(59) = "listed, and indicates that you have
the":A$(60) = "option of going to various places or"
530 A$(61) = "objects. The game opens with your":A$(62)
= "character at his computer, which is in"
531 A$(63) = "the living room. If you leave the":A$(64)
= "computer (to " +  CHR$ (34) + "GO TO WINDOW" +  CHR$
(34) + ", for"
```

532 A$(65) = "example), you can get back by entering":A$
(66) = "either " + CHR$ (34) + "GO TO COMPUTER" + CHR$
(34) + " or " + CHR$ (34) + "GO TO"
533 A$(67) = "DESK" + CHR$ (34) + ". If you leave the
living room,":A$(68) = "you can return with " + CHR$
(34) + "GO TO LIVING"
534 A$(69) = "ROOM" + CHR$ (34) + ", " + CHR$ (34) +
"GO TO COMPUTER" + CHR$ (34) + " or " + CHR$ (34) +
"GO TO":A$(70) = "DESK" + CHR$ (34) + ". All other
things/places that you"
535 A$(71) = "can GO TO from your current
position":A$(72) = "are named when you enter " + CHR$
(34) + "LOOK AROUND" + CHR$ (34) + "."
536 A$(73) = "Sometimes you will see " + CHR$ (34) +
"PLUS OTHER" + CHR$ (34) + "":A$(74) = "listed as an
option. This indicates"
537 A$(75) = "that certain " + CHR$ (34) + "hidden" +
CHR$ (34) + " options are open.":A$(76) = "Usually you
can find out what they are"
538 A$(77) = "by " + CHR$ (34) + "LOOKing AROUND" +
CHR$ (34) + ". Because the action":A$(78) = "(this is "
+ CHR$ (34) + "action" + CHR$ (34) + "??) in Terminal"
539 A$(79) = "Boredom is confined to three rooms,
you":A$(80) = "shouldn't need a map to keep track of"
540 A$(81) = "where you are. You might find it":A$(82) =
"helpful, however, to take notes on the"
541 A$(83) = "sequence of things you do each time
you":A$(84) = "play."
542 A$(85) = "   ":A$(86) = "When the game responds with
the " + CHR$ (34) + "Sorry,"
543 A$(87) = "I can't decipher your input . . ." + CHR$
(34) + "":A$(88) = "message, it means one of the
following:"
544 A$(89) = "You may have tried to do something
that":A$(90) = "isn't allowed at your present position"
545 A$(91) = "in the game. (For example, you
can't":A$(92) = "" + CHR$ (34) + "GET" + CHR$ (34) + "
something that's in the bedroom"
546 A$(93) = "if you're in the living room.) You may":A$
(94) = "have tried to do something that isn't"
547 A$(95) = "allowed in the game at all. (You can't":A$
(96) = "catch a plane to Bermuda, for example.)"

21

548 A$(97) = "Or you may simply have made a typing":A$(98) = "mistake."
549 A$(99) = "   ":A$(100) = "Terminal Boredom is a pretty quick"
550 A$(101) = "little game as computer adventure games":A$(102) = "go. Unless you're a very slow typist,"
551 A$(103) = "playing the game through to a " + CHR$ (34) + "lose" + CHR$ (34) + "":A$(104) = "situation will take minutes, rather"
552 A$(105) = "than hours (or days, weeks, months, . .":A$(106) = ".). As for how long it will take to"
553 A$(107) = "find your way through to a " + CHR$ (34) + "win" + CHR$ (34) + " . . .":A$(108) = "well, that all depends. There's more"
554 A$(109) = "than one way to win at Terminal":A$(110) = "Boredom; there's a bunch of ways to"
555 A$(111) = "lose. If you decide you've had enough":A$(112) = "and want end it all, just type in"
556 A$(113) = "something ending with " + CHR$ (34) + "SLEEP" + CHR$ (34) + ".":A$(114) = " "
557 A$(115) = "A " + CHR$ (34) + "female protagonist" + CHR$ (34) + " version of T.B.":A$(116) = "may be available by the time you read"
558 A$(117) = "this. If you'd prefer that version, ask":A$(118) = "for it when you send me the $5.00"
559 A$(119) = "   ":A$(120) = "REALLY BORING TECHNICAL STUFF: "
560 A$(121) = "Terminal Boredom will run on Apple II":A$(122) = "family computers. Because it uses a"
561 A$(123) = "" + CHR$ (34) + "moved" + CHR$ (34) + " DOS (loaded into the top 16K":A$(124) = "RAM or language card), it requires at"
562 A$(125) = "least 64K, and Applesoft in ROM. ":A$(126) = " "
563 A$(127) = "If you should find a bug in this disk":A$(128) = "and can describe it to me, and it's one"
564 A$(129) = "that I haven't already fixed, or if you":A$(130) = "give me a suggestion for improving"
565 A$(131) = "Terminal Boredom that I decide to use,":A$(132) = "I'll reward you with a refund of the"

566 A$(133) = "above-mentioned $5.00. On the other":A$(134) = "hand, if your copy of this disk crashes"
567 A$(135) = "or is otherwise seriously screwed up,":A$(136) = "it's probably because someone has"
568 A$(137) = "tinkered with it in some way. (It":A$(138) = "worked okay when it left my hands,"
569 A$(139) = "honest!) Let me know when you send the":A$(140) = "$5.00, and I'll send you a working"
570 A$(141) = "copy.":A$(142) = "   "
571 A$(143) = "To prevent any casual cheating,":A$(144) = "Terminal Boredom is (slightly)"
572 A$(145) = "protected against LISTing. If you're":A$(146) = "going to cheat, you'll have to put some"
573 A$(147) = "forethought into it.":A$(148) = "   "
574 A$(149) = "This disk contains a high-speed":A$(150) = "operating system called Diversi-"
575 A$(151) = "DOS(tm), which is licensed for use with":A$(152) = "this program only. To legally use"
576 A$(153) = "Diversi-DOS with other programs, you":A$(154) = "may send $30 directly to: DSR, Inc.,"
577 A$(155) = "34880 Bunker Hill, Farmington, MI":A$(156) = "48018. You will receive a Diversi-DOS"
578 A$(157) = "utility disk with documentation.":A$(158) = "   "
579 A$(159) = "And of course, Terminal Boredom is":A$(160) = "copyrighted, 1986; Karl Bunker, Bunker-"
580 A$(161) = "Stark Industries. No warranties,":A$(162) = "express or implied, blah blah blah,"
581 A$(163) = "etc., etc.":A$(164) = "   "
582 A$(165) = "Tally ho; happy boredom!":A$(166) = "   "
583 A$(167) = "   ":A$(168) = " *p*l*u*g*p*l*u*g*p*l*u*g*p*l*u*g*"
584 A$(169) = "   ":A$(170) = "Also from Bunker-Stark Industries: "
585 A$(171) = "Say! Are you sick of wimpy, mealy-":A$(172) = "mouthed, simpering, " + CHR$ (34) + "user friendly" + CHR$ (34) + ""
586 A$(173) = "software? Are you tired of programs":A$(174) = "that are always being cheerful and"
587 A$(175) = "helpful, and constantly saying stupid":A$(176) = "things like " + CHR$ (34) + "please" + CHR$

23

(34) + " and " + CHR$ (34) + "thank you" + CHR$ (34) +
""
588 A$(177) = "and " + CHR$ (34) + "I'm sorry. . ." +
CHR$ (34) + "? Then you're ready":A$(178) = "for
Eliza*Brat! Eliza*Brat is a highly"
589 A$(179) = "sophisticated A.I. (Artificial":A$(180) =
"Insubordination) program that can"
590 A$(181) = "" + CHR$ (34) + "converse" + CHR$ (34)
+ " with you on any subject at":A$(182) = "all. However,
for some reason (probably"
591 A$(183) = "an unhappy childhood),
Eliza*Brat's":A$(184) = "favorite subject is how little
she"
592 A$(185) = "thinks of you, how stupid she
thinks":A$(186) = "you are, how much she'd rather not
be"
593 A$(187) = "talking to you, etc., etc. If
you're":A$(188) = "anxious to be abused and humiliated
by"
594 A$(189) = "your computer, then Eliza*Brat is
what":A$(190) = "you're looking for! Also on the"
595 A$(191) = "Eliza*Brat disk is a bunch of
more":A$(192) = "serious-minded stuff, including what
is"
596 A$(193) = "probably the most sophisticated":A$(194)
= "" + CHR$ (34) + "straight" + CHR$ (34) + " Eliza-
type program available"
597 A$(195) = "for Apple IIs. The disk is available
as":A$(196) = "Shareware, or order direct by sending"
598 A$(197) = "$7.00 to Karl Bunker at the
address":A$(198) = "above."
600 RETURN

TERMINAL.BOREDOM.BAS

ROW,

ROW,

ROW YOUR BOAT,

GENTLY DOWN THE STREAM...
```
{^D}RUN TERMINAL.BOREDOM
15 MAXFILES = 1: HOME : IF  NOT ( PEEK (103) = 1 AND
PEEK (104) = 96) THEN  PRINT : PRINT  CHR$ (4)"RUN
MENU.DOCS"
20  PRINT : PRINT  CHR$ (4)"BLOAD PK,A2050": POKE
49239,0: POKE 49234,0
25  PRINT : PRINT  CHR$ (4)"BLOAD TERM.SH,A3050": POKE
232,234: POKE 233,11: POKE 230,32: ROT= 0: SCALE= 1
30 P2 = 11: PRINT  CHR$ (4)"BLOAD TB.11.P": POKE
49232,0: CALL 2050: POKE 49168,0: FOR I = 1 TO 700
35  IF  PEEK (49152) > 128 GOTO 45
40  NEXT I
45  TEXT : HOME : FOR I = 1 TO 400: NEXT
50  POKE 49235,0: POKE 49168,0:EF = 1:SX = 19
55 BL$(1) = "STILL KIND OF BORED.":BL$(2) = "STILL
PRETTY BORED.":BL$(3) = "PRETTY DARN BORED.":BL$(4) =
"REALLY, REALLY, REALLY BORED."
60 ES$ = "!":L$ = "|": IF  PEEK (64435) <  > 6 THEN L$ =
"!"
65  GOTO 415
70  REM
SUBROUTINE SANDWICHES

75  REM
DRAW COFFEE

80  HCOLOR= 4: DRAW 1 AT 50,130: HCOLOR= 7: DRAW 2 AT
51,121: HCOLOR= 5: DRAW 3 AT 52,130
85 JT = 1: RETURN
90  REM
```

DRAW BEER

```
95  HCOLOR= 3: DRAW 5 AT 11,83: HCOLOR= 1: DRAW 4 AT
8,83: HCOLOR= 0: DRAW 6 AT 8,81
100 BT = 1: RETURN
105  REM
DRAW LITTLE IIC

110  HCOLOR= 3: DRAW 7 AT 25,83: HCOLOR= 4: DRAW 9 AT
25,83
115 CT = 1: RETURN
120  REM
DRAW LITTLE IIE

125  HCOLOR= 3: DRAW 8 AT 20,71: HCOLOR= 4: DRAW 10 AT
20,71
130 ET = 1: RETURN
135  REM
INPUT QUERY

140  POKE 32,0: POKE 33,28: HTAB 1: VTAB 24
145  IF SC = SX - 4 AND  NOT SW GOTO 2105
150  IF SC = SX GOTO 2120
155  IF NC THEN NC = NC + 1: REM  NC>2 HANDLED UNDER
CHAP.5, STP.6
160  IF OW THEN OW = OW + 1: IF OW > 3 GOTO 1585
165 GQ = 0:QF = 0:Q =  FRE (0): POKE 32,0: POKE 33,28:
HTAB 1: VTAB 24
170  PRINT " WHAT WOULD YOU LIKE TO DO?": PRINT : PRINT
175 I2$ = IN$:IN$ = ""
180  GET G$: IF  ASC (G$) > 31 AND  ASC (G$) < 123 AND
LEN (IN$) < 27 THEN  PRINT G$;
185  IF  ASC (G$) > 96 THEN G$ =  CHR$ ( ASC (G$) - 32)
190  IF  ASC (G$) > 31 AND  ASC (G$) < 91 AND  LEN (IN$)
< 35 THEN IN$ = IN$ + G$
195  IF G$ =  CHR$ (95) OR G$ =  CHR$ (8) THEN G$ =
CHR$ (8): IF  LEN (IN$) = 1 THEN  PRINT G$;: CALL  -
868:IN$ = ""
200  IF G$ =  CHR$ (8) AND  LEN (IN$) > 1 THEN  PRINT
CHR$ (8);: CALL  - 868:IN$ =  LEFT$ (IN$, LEN (IN$) - 1)
205  IF G$ =  CHR$ (2) THEN  END
210  IF G$ <  > CHR$ (13) AND  LEN (IN$) < 35 GOTO 180
215  PRINT : PRINT
```

```
220   IF  LEN (IN$) < 3 GOTO 170
225   IF  RIGHT$ (IN$,1) = " " OR  RIGHT$ (IN$,1) = "."
OR  RIGHT$ (IN$,1) = "!" THEN IN$ =  LEFT$ (IN$, LEN
(IN$) - 1): GOTO 220
230   ON PL GOTO 455,1035,1235,1435,1595,1755,2020
235   REM
WORD WRAP FOR OUTPUT

240   PRINT : GOSUB 245: PRINT : PRINT : RETURN
245 W =  PEEK (33): VTAB 23
250   IF  LEN (A$) > W - 1 GOTO 260
255   PRINT " "A$;: RETURN
260   FOR L = W - 1 TO 2 STEP  - 1:SP$ =  MID$ (A$,L,1)
265   IF SP$ = " " THEN SP = 1: GOTO 280
270   IF SP$ = "-" AND L < W - 1 THEN SP = 0: GOTO 280
275   NEXT L
280 FR$ =  LEFT$ (A$,L - SP): PRINT " "FR$
285 R =  LEN (A$) - ( LEN (FR$) + SP)
290   IF R > 0 THEN A$ =  RIGHT$ (A$,R): GOTO 250
295   RETURN
300   REM
SET UP RIGHT WINDOW

305   POKE 33,11: POKE 32,29: HOME : VTAB 2
310   PRINT "YOU CAN:": PRINT : PRINT
315   PRINT "GO TO _ _": PRINT : RETURN
320   REM
HGR1,BLOAD PIX, SET UP WINDOWS, CURSOR IN LEFT

330   IF P2 = P AND (BC < (BT) OR JF < JT) THEN P2 = 0
335   IF P2 < > P THEN  PRINT : PRINT  CHR$ (4)"BLOAD
TB."P".P,A$4000":P2 = P: CALL 2050:BT = 0:JT = 0:CT =
0:ET = 0
340   IF P > 10 AND BC AND  NOT BT THEN  GOSUB 90
345   IF P > 10 AND P < > 15 AND JF > JT THEN  GOSUB 75
350   IF P = 2 AND CF > (CT) AND  NOT EF THEN  GOSUB 105
355   IF P = 2 AND EF > ET THEN  GOSUB 120
360   TEXT : HOME : POKE 49232,0
365 A$ = I$: GOSUB 245: POKE 49168,0
370 K =  PEEK (49152) - 128: IF K < 0 GOTO 370
375   IF K < > 32 AND K < > 13 THEN  POKE 49168,0: GOTO
370
380   POKE 49168,0: IF AD = 2 THEN  RETURN
```

```
385   TEXT : HOME : FOR I = 1 TO 23: HTAB 29: PRINT L$:
NEXT
390   HTAB 29: PRINT L$;: VTAB 22: POKE 33,28: IF  NOT DR
THEN A$ = I$: GOSUB 235
395   RETURN
400   REM
PRINT CHAPTER #

405   IF MC THEN  PRINT " YOU ARE ON CHAPTER "MC: PRINT "
OF THE APPLESOFT BASIC": PRINT " MANUAL. THERE ARE
FIVE": PRINT " CHAPTERS TO THE MANUAL.": PRINT
410   RETURN
415   REM
 OPENING PAGE WITH TB.1

420 PL = 1
425 I$ = "YOU ARE SITTING IN FRONT OF YOUR COMPUTER (AN
APPLE IIE), PLAYING AN INCREDIBLY BORING 'ADVENTURE'
GAME; YOU'RE ABOUT TO FALL ASLEEP."
430 BL = 3:P = 11: GOSUB 320: GOSUB 300
435   PRINT "LOOK AROUND"
440   PRINT "PLAY GAME": PRINT
445   PRINT "   ***": PRINT "PLUS OTHER": PRINT "    ***"
450   GOTO 135
455   REM
'AT COMPUTER' ANSWERS

460 LD = 0
465   IF IN$ = "PLAY GAME" THEN LD = 1
470   IF IN$ = "LOOK AROUND" THEN LD = 2
475   IF IN$ = "GO TO KITCHEN" THEN LD = 3
480   IF IN$ = "GO TO BEDROOM" THEN LD = 4
485   IF IN$ = "GO TO BED ROOM" THEN LD = 4
490   IF IN$ = "GO TO WINDOW" THEN LD = 5
495   IF IN$ = "GO TO STEREO" OR IN$ = "GO TO RADIO" THEN
LD = 6
500   IF  LEFT$ (IN$,3) = "GO " AND  RIGHT$ (IN$,4) =
"HONE" THEN LD = 7
505   IF  LEFT$ (IN$,4) = "READ" AND AF AND ((EF) OR CF)
THEN LD = 8
510   IF IN$ = "GET RID OF COFFEE" AND JF THEN LD = 9
515   IF  LEFT$ (IN$,7) = "GET RID" AND ( RIGHT$ (IN$,3)
= "IIE" OR  RIGHT$ (IN$,2) = "2E") AND EF THEN LD = 10
```

```
520   IF IN$ = "GET RID OF BEER" AND BC THEN LD = 11
525   IF IN$ = "GO TO COMPUTER" OR IN$ = "GO TO DESK"
THEN LD = 12:L = 0
530   IF LD = 8 AND (CF AND EF) THEN LD = 12
535   IF LD = 0 GOTO 2130
540   ON LD GOTO
1930,625,1085,1285,1495,1650,1815,670,1960,1960,1960,545
545   REM
BACK AT COMPUTER/LIVING ROOM

550   PL = 1:SC = SC + 1:LL = 0
555   IF CF AND EF THEN A$ = "SORRY, BUT THERE'S NO ROOM
ON YOUR DESK FOR BOTH COMPUTERS. BEFORE YOU CAN GET TO
WORK, YOU'LL HAVE TO GET RID OF THE IIE.": GOSUB 235:
GOSUB 300: GOTO 610
560   IF L THEN A$ = "YOU'RE BACK IN THE LIVING ROOM.":
GOSUB 235: GOSUB 300: GOTO 590
565   IF (EF) OR CF THEN I$ = "YOU'RE BACK AT THE
COMPUTER, AND YOU'RE " + BL$(BL)
570 P = 11: IF CF THEN P = 12
575   IF (EF) OR CF THEN   GOSUB 320
580   IF   NOT ((EF) OR CF) THEN A$ = "YOU'RE BACK AT YOUR
DESK -WITHOUT A COMPUTER.": GOSUB 235
585   GOSUB 300
590   IF (CF) OR EF THEN   PRINT "PLAY GAME": PRINT
595   IF   NOT LL THEN   PRINT "LOOK AROUND"
600   IF AF AND ((EF) OR CF) THEN   PRINT "READ": PRINT
"APPLESOFT": PRINT "MANUAL": PRINT
605   IF   NOT BC AND EF AND   NOT ES THEN   PRINT "   ***":
PRINT "PLUS OTHER": PRINT "   ***": PRINT
610   IF ES OR BC OR (CF AND EF) THEN   PRINT "GET RID":
PRINT "OF _ _": PRINT
615   IF EF AND CF THEN   VTAB 8: PRINT "OF IIE "
620   GOTO 135
625   REM
LOOK AROUND, IN LIVING ROOM

630   GOSUB 635:LL = 1:SC = SC + 1: GOTO 585
635 I$ = "YOU ARE IN A SMALL, BORING, LIVING ROOM. IN
ADDITION TO THE COMPUTER, THERE IS A PHONE, ONE WINDOW
AND A STEREO."
640   IF PL > 3 THEN AD = 2:AD$ =   RIGHT$ (I$,71)
645 P = 1: GOSUB 320: IF AD THEN AD = 1
```

```
650   IF PL > 3 THEN  TEXT : HOME :I$ = "THERE'S A SMALL
DESK FOR YOUR COMPUTER.":P = 2: GOSUB 320
655   IF AD = 1 THEN A$ = AD$: GOSUB 235:AD = 0
660 A$ = "THERE ARE TWO DOORS, ONE LEADING TO THE
KITCHEN AND THE OTHER TO THE BEDROOM."
665   GOSUB 235: RETURN
670   REM
READING ASB MANUAL

675 MC = MC + 1: ON MC GOTO 680,730,800,830,890,935
680   REM
ASB, CHAP. 1

685   IF RO GOTO 1010
690   IF  NOT JF THEN I$ = "OKAY! YOU'VE BEGUN YOUR STUDY
OF APPLESOFT - BUT YOU'VE GOT A LONG GRIND AHEAD OF YOU,
AND YOU'RE ALREADY REALLY BORED.":BL = 4
695   IF JF THEN I$ = "AHA! YOU'RE GETTING STARTED ON
LEARNING BASIC, AND THE COFFEE SHOULD HELP TO KEEP YOU
AWAKE WHILE YOU STUDY.":BL = 2
700   IF ES THEN I$ = "WITH ADMIRABLE DETERMINATION, YOU
ARE STARTING ALL OVER IN YOUR EFFORTS TO LEARN APPLESOFT
BASIC."
705   IF JF AND EF THEN P = 13
710   IF JF AND CF THEN P = 14
715   IF  NOT JF AND EF THEN P = 11
720   IF  NOT JF AND CF THEN P = 12
725   GOSUB 320: GOSUB 400: GOTO 585
730   REM
ASB, CHAP. 2

735   IF JF AND RO GOTO 1010
740   IF JF AND BC GOTO 985
745   IF  NOT JF THEN A$ = "WHOOPS - SORRY PAL, BUT
TRYING TO STUDY BASIC WITHOUT ANYTHING TO KEEP YOU AWAKE
HAS DONE YOU IN. THE TEDIUM OF IT ALL OVERCOMES YOU; YOU
FALL ASLEEP.": GOSUB 235: GOTO 2350
750   IF  NOT CF THEN I$ = "YOU'RE STILL STUDYING BASIC.
YOU'VE TYPED IN SOME PRACTICE PROGRAMS - - OH NO! YOU'VE
SPILLED YOUR COFFEE ONTO YOUR IIE KEYBOARD" + ES$
755   IF CF THEN I$ = "YOU'RE COOKIN' WITH GAS! YOU'VE
GOT YOUR COFFEE AND YOUR IIC AND YOU'RE MAKING PROGRESS
WITH BASIC. YOU'RE ALMOST FEELING AWAKE!"
```

```
760  IF  NOT CF THEN P = 15:BL = 4
765  IF CF THEN P = 14:BL = 1
770  GOSUB 320
775  IF ES THEN A$ = "UH-OH - ANOTHER COFFEE-CAUSED
SHORT IN YOUR IIE HAS WIPED OUT ALL YOUR PRACTICE
PROGRAMS AGAIN. IT'S MORE THAN YOU CAN TAKE. APATHY
OVERTAKES YOU AND YOU CRAWL OFF TO BED.": GOSUB 235:
GOTO 2350
780  IF  NOT CF THEN A$ = "THIS CAUSES AN UNUSUAL SHORT
CIRCUIT WHICH DOESN'T DAMAGE THE IIE, BUT WHICH ERASES
ALL YOUR PRACTICE PROGRAMS. THIS SETS YOU BACK TO
'SQUARE ONE' IN YOUR STUDIES. YOU'RE GETTING PRETTY
BORED AND FRUSTRATED."
785  IF CF THEN A$ = "AND BY THE WAY, YOU DON'T HAVE TO
WORRY ABOUT SPILLING COFFEE ONTO YOUR KEYBOARD, BECAUSE
THE IIC KEYBOARD IS SPILLAGE-PROOF."
790  IF  NOT CF THEN MC = 0:ES = 1:ES$ = " AGAIN!!"
795  GOSUB 235: GOSUB 400: GOTO 585
800  REM
ASB, CHAP. 3

805  IF RO GOTO 1010
810  IF BC GOTO 985
815  IF  NOT PO THEN I$ = "YOU'RE STILL WORKING AWAY AT
THE APPLESOFT MANUAL, LEARNING ABOUT FOR-NEXT LOOPS - -
OOP! - THE PHONE IS RINGING. . .":PC = 1:P = 14:BL = 3
820  IF PO THEN I$ = "YOU'RE STILL GRINDING AWAY AT THE
MANUAL, BUT TRYING TO FIGURE OUT MULTI-DIMENSIONAL
ARRAYS IS DRIVING YOU UP THE WALL.":P = 12:WF = 3:BL = 4
825  GOSUB 320: GOSUB 400: GOTO 585
830  REM
ASB, CHAP. 4

835  IF RO GOTO 1010
840  IF BC = 2 GOTO 985: REM  BC = 1 ALLOWED FOR BELOW
845 I$ = "THINGS ARE LOOKING UP. MULTI-DIMENSIONAL
ARRAYS ARE STARTING TO MAKE SENSE, AND YOU'RE MAKING
PROGRESS AGAIN.":P = 14:BL = 2
850  IF PC THEN I$ = "YOU'RE TRYING TO READ THE
APPLESOFT MANUAL, BUT THE PHONE IS STILL RINGING AND
MAKING IT QUITE IMPOSSIBLE TO CONCENTRATE."
```

```
855  IF PO OR NC THEN I$ = "YOU'RE BACK TO WORK WITH THE
MANUAL, AND YOU'RE BEGINNING TO FIGURE OUT MULTI-
DIMENSIONAL ARRAYS."
860  IF WF = 3 THEN I$ = "LEARNING APPLESOFT IS GETTING
TO BE REALLY TEDIOUS AND AGGRAVATING. COFFEE ISN'T
ENOUGH TO KEEP YOU AWAKE ANY MORE. YOU'RE ABOUT TO FALL
ASLEEP.":WF = 2
865  IF BC THEN I$ = "NOTHING LIKE A QUICK BEER TO
IMPROVE YOUR OUTLOOK ON LIFE, BUT IT'S ALSO MAKING YOU
DROWSY, AND YOU'RE FEELING REALLY BORED AND
LISTLESS.":BC = 2
870  IF PC OR BC OR WF = 2 THEN P = 12:BL = 4
875  GOSUB 320
880  IF PC THEN A$ = "YOU'RE GETTING REALLY BORED AND
IRRITATED AND ARE ABOUT TO CHUCK EVERYTHING AND GO TO
SLEEP.": GOSUB 235
885  GOSUB 400: GOTO 585
890  REM
ASB, CHAP. 5

895  IF DC = 2 GOTO 1010
900  IF BC = 2 GOTO 985
905  IF NC > 2 GOTO 1920
910  IF PC THEN A$ = "WELL, THAT ENDLESSLY RINGING PHONE
HAS DRIVEN YOU TO DISTRACTION. YOU'VE HAD IT. LASSITUDE
OVERPOWERS YOU AND YOU GO TO SLEEP.": GOSUB 235: GOTO
2350
915  IF WF = 2 THEN A$ = "PHOOEY. EVEN IF YOU'RE
GUZZLING COFFEE, JUST SITTING AT A COMPUTER TRYING TO
LEARN BASIC GETS TO BE ALTOGETHER TOO BORING AFTER A
WHILE. SMOTHERED BY ENNUI, YOU SUCCUMB TO
INSENSIBILITY.": GOSUB 235: GOTO 2350
920 I$ = "YOU'RE BACK ON TRACK NOW; YOU'RE HARD AT WORK
AND ALMOST FINISHED WITH THE APPLESOFT MANUAL!":P =
14:BL = 1
925  IF NC THEN I$ = "YOU'RE STILL BANGING AWAY AT THE
APPLESOFT MANUAL, TRYING TO FIGURE OUT THE MEMORY
MAP.":P = 12:BL = 4
930  GOSUB 320: GOSUB 400: GOTO 585
935  REM
ASB STEP 6; GAME WON!

940  IF NC > 2 GOTO 1920
```

```
945 I$ = "WELL, YOU FINALLY MADE IT! YOU'VE FINISHED THE
MANUAL, RUNNING THE GAUNTLET OF BOREDOM, FATIGUE AND
MISCELLANEOUS HOUSEHOLD HAZARDS."
950 P = 10:DR = 1: GOSUB 320
955 A$ = "YOU HAVE OVERCOME MULTI-TUDINOUS OBSTACLES AND
ACHIEVED THE FORMIDABLE GOAL OF A WORKING KNOW-LEDGE OF
APPLESOFT BASIC. NEVER AGAIN WILL YOU HAVE TO WASTE YOUR
TIME PLAY-ING STUPID 'ADVENTURE/ STRATEGY' GAMES!":
PRINT : GOSUB 235
960 A$ = "AND NEVER AGAIN WILL YOU HAVE TO SUFFER FROM
TERM-INAL BOREDOM, AS LONG AS YOU HAVE A COMPUTER. NOW
YOU CAN DO UN-BORING THINGS LIKE WRITING YOUR OWN STUPID
'ADVENTURE/ STRATEGY' GAMES!": GOSUB 235: PRINT : PRINT
965  POKE 33,11: POKE 32,29: HOME : VTAB 2
970  PRINT "YOU CAN:": PRINT : PRINT
975  PRINT "PAT YOUR-": PRINT "SELF ON": PRINT "THE
BACK!": PRINT
980  PRINT "PLAY AGAIN": GOTO 2390
985  REM
DRINKING BEER WHILE TRYING TO READ ASB MANUAL

990  IF BC = 2 THEN A$ = "WOOPS - - TOO MUCH BEER ON TOP
OF TOO MUCH BOREDOM HAS FINISHED YOU OFF . . . YOU SLIP
INTO A BENUMBED AND BESOTTED STUPOR.": GOSUB 235: GOTO
2350
995  IF BC = 1 THEN I$ = "YOU'RE TRYING TO STUDY THE
APPLESOFT MANUAL, BUT YOU CAN'T RESIST AN OCCASIONAL
BELT FROM THAT BEER, AND IT'S MAKING YOU SLEEPY.":BC =
2:MC = MC - 1
1000 BL = 3:P = 11: IF CF THEN P = 12
1005  GOSUB 320: GOTO 585
1010  REM
RADIO PLAYING WHILE TRYING TO READ ASB MANUAL

1015  IF DC = 2 THEN A$ = "THAT'S IT - IT'S ALL OVER;
TRYING TO LEARN APPLESOFT WITH DISTRACTING MUSIC PLAYING
ON THE RADIO WAS TOO MUCH FOR YOU. APATHY ROUTES
INDUSTRY AND YOU SOON FALL ASLEEP.": GOSUB 235: GOTO
2350
1020 I$ = "YOU'RE TRYING TO LEARN APPLESOFT, BUT THE
RADIO IS ON AND THE NOISE WON'T LET YOU CONCENTRATE.
YOU'RE ABOUT TO GIVE UP AND GO TO SLEEP.":MC = MC - 1:DC
= 2
```

```
1025 BL = 4:P = 11: IF CF THEN P = 12
1030  GOSUB 320: GOTO 585
1035  REM
'IN KITCHEN' ANSWERS

1040 KD = 0
1045  IF IN$ = "LOOK AROUND" THEN KD = 1
1050  IF  LEFT$ (IN$,12) = "GO TO LIVING" OR IN$ = "GO
TO DOOR" THEN KD = 2:L = 1
1055  IF IN$ = "GO TO COMPUTER" OR IN$ = "GO TO DESK"
THEN KD = 3:L = 0
1060  IF  LEFT$ (IN$,11) = "LOOK IN REF" THEN KD = 4
1065  IF IN$ = "GET BEER" AND  NOT BC THEN KD = 5
1070  IF IN$ = "GET COFFEE" AND  NOT JF THEN KD = 6
1075  IF KD = 0 GOTO 2130
1080  ON KD GOTO 1155,545,545,1180,1200,1220
1085  REM
IN KITCHEN

1090  IF TR GOTO 2080
1095  PRINT " YOU ARE IN THE KITCHEN.": PRINT
1100 SC = SC + 1:PL = 2:LK = 0
1105  GOSUB 300
1110  IF  NOT LK THEN  PRINT "LOOK AROUND"
1115  IF BC AND JF THEN LK = 1
1120  IF  NOT LK GOTO 1150
1125  IF  NOT (BC OR LF) THEN  PRINT "LOOK IN": PRINT
"REFRIGERA-": PRINT "TOR": PRINT
1130  IF  NOT JF THEN  PRINT "GET COFFEE": PRINT
1135  IF  NOT BC AND LF THEN  PRINT "GET BEER": PRINT
1140  IF  NOT LF GOTO 1150
1145  GOTO 135
1150  PRINT "   ***": PRINT "PLUS OTHER": PRINT "
***": GOTO 135
1155  REM
LOOK AROUND, IN KITCHEN

1160 I$ = "YOU ARE IN A BARE, SMALL, BORING KITCHEN.
THERE IS A REFRIGERATOR AND A STOVE. ON THE STOVE THERE
IS A POT OF COFFEE."
1165 P = 3: GOSUB 320
1170 A$ = "THE ONLY DOOR LEADS BACK TO THE LIVING
ROOM.": GOSUB 235
```

```
1175 SC = SC + 1:LK = 1: GOTO 1105
1180  REM
LOOK INTO REFRIGERATOR

1185 A$ = "THERE IS A SIX-PACK OF BORING BEER IN THE
REFRIGERATOR."
1190  GOSUB 235
1195 SC = SC + 1:LF = 1: GOTO 1105
1200  REM
GET BEER

1205 A$ = "YOU'VE GOT A NICE COLD, BORING BEER.":BC =
1:LF = 1: GOSUB 235
1210  IF OW OR NC THEN A$ = "MM. THAT BEER WAS JUST WHAT
YOU NEEDED TO LIFT YOUR SPIRITS.": GOSUB 235:OW = 0:NC =
0
1215  GOTO 1105
1220  REM
GET COFFEE

1225 A$ = "YOU'VE GOT A NICE HOT CUP OF COFFEE.":JF = 1
1230  GOSUB 235: GOTO 1105
1235  REM
 'IN BEDROOM' ANSWERS

1240 BD = 0
1245  IF IN$ = "LOOK AROUND" THEN BD = 1
1250  IF  LEFT$ (IN$,12) = "GO TO LIVING" OR IN$ = "GO
TO DOOR" THEN BD = 2:L = 1:BK = 1
1255  IF IN$ = "GO TO COMPUTER" OR IN$ = "GO TO DESK"
THEN BD = 3:L = 0:BK = 1
1260  IF  LEFT$ (IN$,3) = "GET" AND  RIGHT$ (IN$,3) =
"UAL" AND  NOT AF THEN BD = 4
1265  IF  LEFT$ (IN$,3) = "GET" AND  RIGHT$ (IN$,1) =
"C" AND  NOT CF THEN BD = 5
1270  IF  LEFT$ (IN$,4) = "READ" THEN LD = 6
1275  IF BD = 0 GOTO 2130
1280  ON BD GOTO 1345,545,545,1375,1375,1425
1285  REM
 IN BEDROOM

1290  IF TR GOTO 2080
1295  PRINT " YOU ARE IN THE BEDROOM.": PRINT
```

```
1300 SC = SC + 1:PL = 3:LB = 0
1305  GOSUB 300
1310  IF (AF) OR CF THEN LB = 1
1315  PRINT : IF  NOT LB THEN  PRINT "LOOK AROUND":
PRINT
1320  IF  NOT LB AND BD < 4 THEN  PRINT "   ***": PRINT
"PLUS OTHER": PRINT "   ***"
1325  IF  NOT LB GOTO 135
1330  IF  NOT AF AND BK < 4 THEN  PRINT "GET APPLE-":
PRINT "SOFT MANUAL": PRINT
1335  IF  NOT CF AND BK < 4 THEN  PRINT "GET": PRINT
"APPLE IIC": PRINT
1340  GOTO 135
1345  REM
LOOK AROUND, IN BEDROOM

1350 I$ = "YOU ARE IN A SMALL, BORING BEDROOM. THERE IS
A BIG, SOFT, WARM, EXCRUCIATINGLY INVITING BED, AND A
BOOKCASE."
1355 P = 4: GOSUB 320
1360 A$ = "THERE ARE ONLY TWO THINGS IN THE BOOKCASE:
ANOTHER COMPUTER (AN APPLE IIC), AND AN APPLESOFT BASIC
INSTRUCTION MANUAL. THE ONLY DOOR LEADS BACK TO THE
LIVING ROOM."
1365  GOSUB 235
1370 SC = SC + 1:LB = 1: GOTO 1305
1375  REM
GETTING STUFF IN BEDROOM

1380  IF  NOT RO GOTO 1415
1385  IF BD = 4 AND BK = 5 OR BD = 5 AND BK = 4 THEN A$
= "SORRY, BUT YOU CAN'T CARRY BOTH AT ONCE.": GOSUB
235:BD = BK:AF = 0:CF = 0
1390  IF BD = 4 THEN A$ = "YOU'VE GOT THE APPLESOFT
MANUAL":BK = BD:AF = 1
1395  IF BD = 5 THEN A$ = "YOU'VE GOT THE APPLE IIC":BK
= BD:CF = 1
1400  GOSUB 235
1405  IF  NOT RM THEN A$ = "IT'S A GOOD THING YOU'VE GOT
THE RADIO ON. IF IT WEREN'T FOR ALL THAT NOISE, YOU
PROBABLY WOULDN'T BE ABLE TO RESIST DIVING ONTO THE BED
AND GOING TO SLEEP.": GOSUB 235:RM = 1
1410  GOTO 1305
```

```
1415 A$ = "WOOPS! IN YOUR PRESENT STATE OF FATIGUE AND
BOREDOM (AND WITH NOTHING GOING ON TO DISTRACT YOU AND
KEEP YOU AWAKE), THAT NICE SOFT BED WAS SIMPLY
IRRESISTIBLE! YOU'VE COLLAPSED ONTO THE BED."
1420  GOSUB 235: GOTO 2350
1425 A$ = "IT WASN'T AT ALL A GOOD IDEA TO TRY TO DO
SOMETHING AS BORING AS STUDYING BASIC WHILE IN THE SAME
ROOM WITH THAT NICE SOFT BED! YOU LASTED ABOUT TEN
SECONDS BEFORE GIVING IN TO ITS COMFY ATTRACTION AND
GOING TO SLEEP."
1430  GOSUB 235: GOTO 2350
1435  REM
'AT WINDOW' ANSWERS

1440 WD = 0
1445  IF  LEFT$ (IN$,8) = "LOOK OUT" THEN WD = 1
1450  IF IN$ = "GO TO COMPUTER" OR IN$ = "GO TO DESK"
THEN WD = 2:L = 0
1455  IF IN$ = "GO TO BEDROOM" THEN WD = 3
1460  IF IN$ = "GO TO KITCHEN" THEN WD = 4
1465  IF IN$ = "GO TO STEREO" OR IN$ = "GO TO RADIO"
THEN WD = 5
1470  IF  LEFT$ (IN$,3) = "GO " AND  RIGHT$ (IN$,4) =
"HONE" THEN WD = 6
1475  IF  LEFT$ (IN$,5) = "THROW" AND CC THEN WD = 7
1480  IF  LEFT$ (IN$,2) = "GO" AND CC THEN WD = 0
1485  IF WD = 0 GOTO 2130
1490  ON WD GOTO 1540,545,1285,1085,1650,1815,1565
1495  REM
AT WINDOW

1500  PRINT " YOU ARE AT THE WINDOW.": PRINT
1505 SC = SC + 1:PL = 4:LL = 0
1510  GOSUB 300
1515  IF CC THEN  VTAB 5
1520  IF  NOT LL THEN  PRINT "LOOK AROUND"
1525  PRINT "LOOK OUT ": PRINT "WINDOW": PRINT
1530  IF CC THEN  PRINT "THROW IIE": PRINT "OUT WINDOW":
PRINT
1535  GOTO 135
1540  REM
LOOK OUT WINDOW
```

```
1545 I$ = "THERE'S NOTHING MUCH HAPPENING OUTSIDE THE
WINDOW.": IF WF THEN WF = 1
1550 P = 5: GOSUB 320
1555  IF SC > SX - 4 OR WF THEN A$ = "BUT EVEN SO,
LOOKING OUT A WINDOW FOR A WHILE IS A BIT OF A CHANGE OF
PACE, AND YOU FEEL A LITTLE LESS BORED.":SC = SC - 5:BL
= 2: GOSUB 235
1560  GOTO 1505
1565  REM
THROW IIE OUT WINDOW

1570 A$ = "OUT THE WINDOW IT GOES!! (HOPE IT DOESN'T HIT
ANYONE.)": GOSUB 235
1575 A$ = "REASONABLY ENOUGH, THIS IMPULSIVE AND WANTON
DESTRUCTION OF A FINE COMPUTER LEAVES YOU RATHER
DEPRESSED AND DISCOURAGED. YOU'RE ABOUT TO GIVE UP AND
GO TO SLEEP."
1580  GOSUB 235:CC = 0:OW = 1:BL = 4: GOTO 1505
1585 A$ = "YOU'RE STILL REALLY DEPRESSED ABOUT TRASHING
YOUR IIE, AND YOU HAVEN'T DONE ANYTHING TO IMPROVE YOUR
MOOD. YOU'VE GIVEN UP AND YOU GO TO SLEEP."
1590  GOSUB 235: GOTO 2350
1595  REM
'AT STEREO' ANSWERS

1600 SD = 0
1605  IF IN$ = "TURN ON RADIO" THEN SD = 1:RN = 1:RF = 0
1610  IF IN$ = "TURN OFF RADIO" THEN SD = 2:RF = 1:RN =
0
1615  IF IN$ = "GO TO COMPUTER" OR IN$ = "GO TO DESK"
THEN SD = 3:L = 0
1620  IF IN$ = "GO TO BEDROOM" OR IN$ = "GO TO BED ROOM"
THEN SD = 4
1625  IF IN$ = "GO TO KITCHEN" THEN SD = 5
1630  IF IN$ = "GO TO WINDOW" THEN SD = 6
1635  IF  LEFT$ (IN$,3) = "GO " AND  RIGHT$ (IN$,4) =
"HONE" THEN SD = 7
1640  IF SD = 0 GOTO 2130
1645  ON SD GOTO 1695,1695,545,1285,1085,1495,1815
1650  REM
AT STEREO

1655  IF TR GOTO 2080
```

```
1660  PRINT " YOU ARE AT THE STEREO.": PRINT
1665 SC = SC + 1:PL = 5:LL = 0
1670  GOSUB 300
1675  IF  NOT LL THEN  PRINT "LOOK AROUND"
1680  IF  NOT RO THEN  PRINT "TURN ON": PRINT "RADIO":
PRINT : GOTO 135
1685  PRINT "TURN OFF": PRINT "RADIO": PRINT
1690  GOTO 135
1695  REM
RADIO ON/OFF

1700  IF RC = 2 OR DC = 2 GOTO 1730
1705  IF  NOT RO AND RF THEN A$ = "BUT THE RADIO ISN'T
ON!": GOTO 1725
1710  IF RO AND RN THEN A$ = "BUT THE RADIO IS ALREADY
ON!": GOTO 1725
1715  IF RN THEN A$ = "THE RADIO IS TURNED ON.":RO =
1:RC = RC + 1
1720  IF RF THEN A$ = "THE RADIO IS TURNED OFF.":RO =
0:RC = RC + 1
1725  GOSUB 235: GOTO 1665
1730  REM
RADIO SHORT

1735 I$ = "YEEEEE-OOUUUUCH!!! - THERE'S A SHORT CIRCUIT
IN THE RADIO WHICH GIVES YOU A TERRIFIC SHOCK!"
1740 P = 8: GOSUB 320
1745 A$ = "YOU'VE BEEN DONE IN BY A FAULTY STEREO. THE
SHOCK HALF-SCRAMBLES YOUR BRAINS, AND ALL THE FUSES IN
THE HOUSE ARE BLOWN, MAKING IT IMPOSSIBLE TO PLAY WITH
THE COMPUTER. DISORIENTED AND DISCOURAGED, YOU GO TO
BED."
1750  GOSUB 235: GOTO 2350
1755  REM
'AT PHONE' ANSWERS

1760 PD = 0
1765  IF IN$ = "ANSWER PHONE" THEN PD = 1
1770  IF IN$ = "MAKE CALL" THEN PD = 2
1775  IF IN$ = "GO TO COMPUTER" OR IN$ = "GO TO DESK"
THEN PD = 3:L = 0
1780  IF IN$ = "GO TO BEDROOM" THEN PD = 4
1785  IF IN$ = "GO TO KITCHEN" THEN PD = 5
```

```
1790   IF IN$ = "GO TO STEREO" OR IN$ = "GO TO RADIO"
THEN PD = 6
1795   IF IN$ = "GO TO WINDOW" THEN PD = 7
1800   IF  RIGHT$ (IN$,8) = "OFF HOOK" THEN PD = 8
1805   IF PD = 0 GOTO 2130
1810   ON PD GOTO 1865,1865,545,1285,1085,1650,1495,1865
1815   REM
AT PHONE

1820   IF TR GOTO 2080
1825   PRINT " YOU ARE AT THE PHONE.": PRINT
1830 SC = SC + 1:PL = 6:LL = 0
1835   GOSUB 300
1840   IF  NOT LL THEN  PRINT "LOOK AROUND"
1845   IF PC THEN  PRINT "ANSWER": PRINT "PHONE": PRINT
1850   IF  NOT PC THEN  PRINT "MAKE CALL": PRINT
1855   IF  NOT PO AND  NOT NC THEN  PRINT "    ***": PRINT
"PLUS OTHER": PRINT "   ***"
1860   GOTO 135
1865   REM
ANSWER PHONE,ETC.

1870   IF PD = 1 AND PC GOTO 1900
1875   IF PD = 1 AND  NOT PC THEN A$ = "BUT THE PHONE
ISN'T RINGING!"
1880   IF PD = 2 AND PC THEN A$ = "YOU CAN'T MAKE A CALL
WHILE THE PHONE IS RINGING!"
1885   IF PD = 8 THEN A$ = "THE PHONE IS OFF THE
HOOK.":PO = 1:PC = 0
1890   IF PD = 2 AND  NOT PC THEN A$ = "SORRY, WHOEVER
YOU WANTED TO CALL DOESN'T ANSWER.":PO = 0
1895   GOSUB 235: GOTO 1830
1900   REM
BAD NEWS ON PHONE

1905 I$ = "IT'S YOUR GIRLFRIEND, SAYING SHE WANTS TO
BREAK UP WITH YOU."
1910 P = 7: GOSUB 320:A$ = "NATURALLY THIS GETS YOU
PRETTY UPSET AND DEPRESSED; YOU'RE ABOUT TO GIVE UP AND
GO TO SLEEP."
1915   GOSUB 235:NC = 1:PC = 0:BL = 4: GOTO 1830
1920 A$ = "THE BAD NEWS YOU GOT ON THE PHONE HAS REALLY
BUMMED YOU OUT, AND YOU HAVEN'T DONE ANYTHING TO IMPROVE
```

YOUR MOOD. DEPRESSED AND APATHETIC, YOU SOON FALL
ASLEEP."

```
1925  GOSUB 235: GOTO 2350
1930  REM
PLAY GAME

1935 P$ = "YOU ARE STILL PLAYING THAT INCREDIBLY BORING
GAME": IF SC > 1 THEN P$ = "YOU ARE PLAYING THAT
INCREDIBLY BORING GAME AGAIN"
1940 SC = SC + 1:GC = GC + 1:BL = 4:P = 11: IF CF THEN P
= 12
1945  IF GC = 1 THEN I$ = P$ + " (I CAN'T IMAGINE WHY),
AND YOU ARE BEGINNING TO NOD OFF.": GOSUB 320: GOTO 585
1950  IF GC = 2 THEN A$ = "THAT WAS A DUMB MOVE! YOU'VE
LET THAT STUPID GAME BLUDGEON YOU TO UNCONSCIOUSNESS
WITH ITS BRUTAL MONOTONY!"
1955  GOSUB 235: IF GC = 2 GOTO 2350
1960  REM
GET RID OF THINGS

1965  IF LD = 9 THEN A$ = "OKAY, THE COFFEE'S GONE.":JF
= 0
1970  IF LD = 11 THEN A$ = "OKAY, YOUR BEER'S GONE.":BC
= 0
1975  IF LD = 10 THEN A$ = "OKAY, YOU'VE PICKED UP THE
IIE; NOW WHERE WOULD YOU LIKE TO GET RID OF IT?":EF = 0
1980  GOSUB 235: IF LD = 10 GOTO 1990
1985  GOTO 585
1990  POKE 33,11: POKE 32,29: HOME : VTAB 2: PRINT "YOU
CAN"
1995  PRINT "GET RID OF": PRINT "THE IIE": PRINT : PRINT
2000  PRINT "ON THE": PRINT "FLOOR": PRINT
2005  PRINT "OUT THE": PRINT "WINDOW": PRINT
2010  PRINT "IN THE": PRINT "BEDROOM"
2015 PL = 7: POKE 32,0: POKE 33,28: VTAB 24: GOTO 175
2020  REM
'GET RID OF IIE' ANSWERS

2025 LD = 0
2030  IF  RIGHT$ (IN$,5) = "FLOOR" THEN LD = 13
2035  IF  RIGHT$ (IN$,6) = "WINDOW" THEN LD = 14
2040  IF  RIGHT$ (IN$,7) = "BEDROOM" THEN LD = 15:PL = 3
2045  IF LD = 0 GOTO 2130
```

```
2050 ES = 0:CC = 1: ON LD - 12 GOTO 2055,1495,2065
2055 A$ = "OKAY, THE COMPUTER IS OUT OF THE WAY ON THE
FLOOR.":CC = 0
2060 TR = 1:PL = 1: GOSUB 235: GOTO 585
2065  PRINT "YOU ARE IN THE BEDROOM.": PRINT
2070 A$ = "WHOOOP! YOU'RE SO BORED AND TIRED THAT THE
BED HAS SEDUCED YOU RIGHT OFF YOUR FEET. YOU'VE DROPPED
THE IIE AND COLLAPSED ONTO THE PILLOWS."
2075  GOSUB 235: GOTO 2350
2080  REM
TRIP OVER IIE

2085 I$ = "WAAAOOOOOOOUUU!! YOU'VE TRIPPED OVER THAT IIE
YOU LEFT ON THE FLOOR!"
2090 P = 6: GOSUB 320
2095 A$ = "THIS RESULTS IN A BONK ON THE HEAD WHICH
(THANKS LARGELY TO YOUR FATIGUED AND UN-MOTIVATED
CONDITION) KNOCKS YOU UNCONSCIOUS."
2100  GOSUB 235:PL = 2: GOTO 2350
2105  REM
WARNING RE. SC COUNTER

2110 A$ = "YOU'VE SPENT A LOT OF TIME WANDERING AROUND
IN YOUR APARTMENT, AND THE INCREDIBLE DREARINESS OF THE
PLACE IS REALLY BEGINNING TO GET TO YOU."
2115 SW = 1:BL = 4: GOSUB 235: GOTO 170
2120 A$ = "AAUGH! YOU'VE SIMPLY HAD ALL YOU CAN STAND OF
WALKING AROUND IN YOUR BORING APARTMENT. THE DRABNESS OF
THE JOINT OVERWHELMS YOU AND YOU'RE HORIZONTAL AND
ASLEEP BEFORE YOU KNOW WHAT HIT YOU."
2125  GOSUB 235:PL = 2: GOTO 2350
2130  REM
GARBAGE COLLECTION FOR BAD ANSWERS

2135  IF  RIGHT$ (IN$,5) = "SLEEP" THEN A$ = "HAD
ENOUGH, HUH? - - OKAY, YOU'RE ASLEEP!": GOSUB 235: GOTO
2350
2140 A$ = "SORRY, BUT I CAN'T DECIPHER YOUR INPUT;
PLEASE TRY AGAIN."
2145  FOR I = 1 TO  LEN (IN$) - 6: IF  MID$ (IN$,I,5) =
" THE " THEN IN$ =  LEFT$ (IN$,I) +  MID$ (IN$,I + 5):
GOTO 230
2150  NEXT I
```

```
2155  IF  LEFT$ (IN$,4) = "THE " THEN IN$ =  MID$ (IN$,
5)
2160  FOR I = 1 TO  LEN (IN$) - 3: IF  MID$ (IN$,I,4) =
"FRID" OR  MID$ (IN$,I,4) = "FRIG" OR  MID$ (IN$,I,4) =
"'FRI" THEN IN$ =  LEFT$ (IN$,I - 1) + "REF": GOTO 230
2165  NEXT I
2170  IF  LEFT$ (IN$,6) = "GO TO " AND  NOT QF THEN  FOR
QF = 6 TO  LEN (IN$):SP$ =  MID$ (IN$,QF,1): IF SP$ = "
" AND QF > 6 THEN IN$ =  LEFT$ (IN$,QF - 1): GOTO 230
2175  IF QF THEN  NEXT QF:QF = 0
2180  IF PL = 1 AND  LEFT$ (IN$,8) = "PUT DOWN" THEN A$
= "OKAY."
2185  IF PL = 4 AND  LEFT$ (IN$,4) = "JUMP" THEN A$ =
"HEY, C'MON! THINGS AREN'T AS BAD AS ALL THAT, ARE
THEY?"
2190  IF PL = 4 AND  LEFT$ (IN$,5) = "CLIMB" THEN A$ =
"SORRY, THAT'S NOT ALLOWED. (YOU WANT TO FALL AND BREAK
YOUR NECK?!)"
2195  IF IN$ = "PLUS OTHER" THEN A$ = "'PLUS OTHER'
ISN'T AN OPTION. IT'S THERE TO LET YOU KNOW THAT CERTAIN
'HIDDEN' OPTIONS ARE OPEN TO YOU."
2200  IF IN$ = "LOOK AROUND" AND PL > 3 AND PL < 7 THEN
GOSUB 635: ON PL - 3 GOTO 1510,1670,1835
2205  IF PL = 5 AND ( RIGHT$ (IN$,6) = "RECORD" OR
RIGHT$ (IN$,4) = "TAPE" OR  MID$ (IN$, LEN (IN$) - 3,3)
= "DIS") THEN A$ = "SORRY, YOU DON'T OWN ANY. ALL YOU'VE
GOT IS THE RADIO."
2210  IF IN$ = "GET RID OF COFFEE" AND  NOT (JF) OR IN$
= "GET RID OF BEER" AND  NOT BC THEN A$ = "BUT YOU DON'T
HAVE ANY!"
2215  IF IN$ = "GET BEER" AND BC OR IN$ = "GET COFFEE"
AND JF THEN A$ = "BUT YOU'VE ALREADY GOT SOME!"
2220  IF  LEFT$ (IN$,5) = "THROW" AND PL = 4 AND  NOT CC
THEN A$ = "BUT YOU HAVEN'T GOT THE IIE!"
2225  IF  LEFT$ (IN$,3) = "GET" AND ( RIGHT$ (IN$,3) =
"UAL" AND (AF) OR  RIGHT$ (IN$,1) = "C" AND CF) THEN A$
= "BUT YOU ALREADY HAVE IT!"
2230  IF IN$ = "DRINK BEER" AND BC OR IN$ = "DRINK
COFFEE" AND JF THEN A$ = "GULP!GULP!"
2235  IF IN$ = "DRINK COFFEE" AND  NOT (JF) OR IN$ =
"DRINK BEER" AND  NOT BC THEN A$ = "BUT YOU HAVEN'T GOT
ANY!"
```

```
2240  IF IN$ = "DRINK BEER" AND BC AND (OW OR NC) THEN
A$ = "SORRY, YOU FINISHED YOUR BEER.": IF OW THEN OW = 1
2245  IF IN$ = "DRINK BEER" AND BC AND (OW OR NC) THEN
BC = 0: IF NC THEN NC = 1
2250  IF IN$ = "GET RID OF IIC" THEN A$ = "SORRY, BUT
THAT'S NOT ALLOWED."
2255  IF  LEFT$ (IN$,10) = "WRITE PROG" THEN A$ = "SORRY
BUT YOU DON'T KNOW ENOUGH BASIC TO DO THAT YET."
2260  IF (IN$ = "LEARN BASIC" OR  LEFT$ (IN$,8) = "LEARN
AP") AND  NOT AF THEN A$ = "HOW? TO LEARN BASIC, YOU'LL
NEED AN INSTRUCTION MANUAL."
2265  IF  LEFT$ (IN$,4) = "READ" AND  NOT ((EF) OR CF)
THEN A$ = "BUT YOU DON'T HAVE A COMPUTER - YOU HAVE TO
HAVE A COMPUTER TO LEARN BASIC."
2270  IF  LEFT$ (IN$,4) = "READ" AND  NOT AF THEN A$ =
"BUT YOU DON'T HAVE ONE!"
2275  REM
MIXED UP 'GO TO _ _'S

2280  IF (PL = 1 OR PL > 3) AND IN$ = "GO TO DOOR" THEN
A$ = "DO YOU WANT TO GO THE KITCHEN OR THE BEDROOM?":GW
= 2: GOTO 2335
2285  IF PL = 2 AND (IN$ = "GO TO STOVE" OR  LEFT$ (IN$,
8) = "GO TO RE") THEN A$ = "OKAY.": GOTO 2345
2290  IF PL = 3 AND IN$ = "GO TO BOOKCASE" THEN A$ =
"OKAY.": GOTO 2345
2295 A2$ = "SORRY, YOU HAVE TO 'GO TO LIVING ROOM'
FIRST."
2300  IF PL = 2 AND IN$ = "GO TO BEDROOM" OR PL = 3 AND
IN$ = "GO TO KITCHEN" THEN A$ = A2$: GOTO 2345
2305  IF (PL = 2 OR PL = 3) AND (IN$ = "GO TO STEREO" OR
IN$ = "GO TO PHONE" OR IN$ = "GO TO WINDOW" OR IN$ = "GO
TO RADIO") THEN A$ = A2$: GOTO 2345
2310  IF  LEN (I2$) < 7 THEN I2$ = "          ": REM
PREVENT ILL. QUANT.
2315  IF  LEFT$ (IN$,5) = "GO TO" AND  NOT GQ THEN A$ =
"GO TO WHERE?":GW = 2:GQ = 1
2320  IF GW = 1 AND  LEFT$ (I2$,5) = "GO TO" AND (IN$ =
I2$ OR IN$ =  RIGHT$ (I2$, LEN (I2$) - 6)) THEN A$ =
"SORRY, YOU CAN'T GO THERE.":GW = 0
2325  IF GW = 1 THEN IN$ = "GO TO " + IN$:GW = 0:QF = 0:
GOTO 230
2330  IF GW = 1 THEN  NEXT
```

```
2335  IF GW THEN GW = GW - 1: GOSUB 235: GOTO 175
2340  REM
FOR MOST OF THE ABOVE:

2345  GOSUB 235: GOTO 165
2350  REM
YOU LOSE, SUCKER

2355  GOSUB 300: VTAB 5
2360  PRINT "LIE THERE": PRINT "AND SLEEP!"
2365  POKE 32,0: POKE 33,28: VTAB 24: HTAB 1: INPUT
"PLEASE PRESS <RETURN>";G$
2370 I$ = "NIGHTY-NIGHT, SLEEPY HEAD!              "
2375 P = 9: IF CF AND PL = 1 THEN P = 16
2380  GOSUB 320: PRINT : PRINT : GOSUB 300: VTAB 5:
PRINT "LIE THERE": PRINT "AND SLEEP"
2385  VTAB 9: PRINT "WAKE YOUR-": PRINT "SELF UP": PRINT
"AND START": PRINT "AGAIN"
2390  POKE 32,0: POKE 33,28
2395 A$ = "PRESS <RETURN> TO START AGAIN, OR ANY OTHER
KEY TO END."
2400  GOSUB 245: GET G$: IF  ASC (G$) = 13 THEN  RUN 45
2405  TEXT : HOME : VTAB 10: PRINT "PRESS ANY KEY TO RE-
BOOT": GET G$
2410  IF  ASC (G$) <  > 2 THEN  CALL  - 1370
```

More from Bunker-Stark Industries

Say! Are you sick of wimpy, mealy-mouthed, simpering, "user friendly" software? Are you tired of programs that are always being cheerful and helpful, and constantly saying stupid things like "please" and "thank you" and "I'm sorry. . ." ?

Then you're ready for Eliza*Brat! Eliza*Brat is a highly sophisticated A.I. (Artificial Insubordination) program that can "converse" with you on any subject at all. However, for some reason (probably an unhappy childhood), Eliza*Brat's favorite subject is how little it thinks of you, how stupid it thinks you are, how much it would rather not be talking to you, etc. If you're anxious to be abused and humiliated by your computer, then Eliza*Brat is what you're looking for!

Also on the Eliza*Brat disk is a bunch of more serious-minded stuff, including what is probably the most sophisticated "straight" Eliza-type program available for the Apple II.